T0197326

Final Act *of* Honor

A GUIDE FOR FAMILIES ABOUT BURIALS AND CREMATIONS

Allan Hunsperger

WESTBOW
PRESS®
A DIVISION OF THOMAS NELSON
& ZONDERVAN

This book is a work of non-fiction. Unless otherwise noted, the author and the publisher make no explicit guarantees as to the accuracy of the information contained in this book and in some cases, names of people and places have been altered to protect their privacy.

WestBow Press books may be ordered through booksellers or by contacting:

WestBow Press
A Division of Thomas Nelson & Zondervan
1663 Liberty Drive
Bloomington, IN 47403
www.westbowpress.com
844-714-3454

Because of the dynamic nature of the Internet, any web addresses or links contained in this book may have changed since publication and may no longer be valid. The views expressed in this work are solely those of the author and do not necessarily reflect the views of the publisher, and the publisher hereby disclaims any responsibility for them.

Any people depicted in stock imagery provided by Getty Images are models, and such images are being used for illustrative purposes only. Certain stock imagery © Getty Images.

Unless otherwise noted, all Scripture quotations are taken from the Holman Christian Standard Bible®, Used by Permission HCSB ©1999,2000,2002,2003,2009 Holman Bible Publishers. Holman Christian Standard Bible®, Holman CSB®, and HCSB® are federally registered trademarks of Holman Bible Publishers.

ISBN: 978-1-6642-2532-9 (sc)
ISBN: 978-1-6642-2533-6 (e)

Print information available on the last page.

WestBow Press rev. date: 05/19/2021

Table of Contents

Endorsements

Thought Provoking…. Informative…. Compelling Pastor Al did a great job of explaining the why of burial in a manner that Christian believers and nonbelievers alike can understand and appreciate. This is a subject that I have been thinking about for years. I am married to a Canadian and live in Canada, while my nuclear family (mother and sisters), and extended family (aunts, uncles, cousins) mostly live in South Carolina. In Southern Baptist family it is a tradition that we are buried with a memorial stone. The cemeteries in my hometown are viewed as sacred grounds. Spoken about with reverence. They are seen as a way of keeping the memory of the deceased alive. I can remember constantly visiting the grave site of my grandfather whenever I had a major decision to make or life challenge. It was therapeutic and kept our spirits connected. So, I appreciated and related to the social and Biblical explanations that Pastor Al presented.

As we all seek knowledge, the question Why seems to always come up. In this book, Pastor Al gave clear examples of why we bury our loved ones, referencing the actions in the book of Genesis. He also gave understandable examples of why people may choose not to do so. Most notably financial reasons. This is particularly reflected in the scholarly way he spoke about the option of cremation. He did not dismiss the practice, one I was considering myself, instead he cited how cremation is not an option in scriptures. That was educational for me as a Christian. This gave me pause for reconsideration of my funeral plans.

This book was a compelling, informative, and thought-provoking piece that everyone can appreciate. Losing a loved one is never easy. There are a lot of emotions that can burden the heart, mind, and body. Pastor Al smartly explained how we can find peace and comfort in how we honor our loved ones through the practice of burial. His non-judgmental approach makes it a read for all regardless of religious beliefs.

Insightful work from a very thoughtful and caring man. I was compelled to change my thinking, and I feel a lot of people in my circle will benefit from this literature. Great work Pastor Al. I can honestly say you are a friend and scholar.

Sincerely,
Kavis Reed

Endorsement by Tyler Weber, President of the Alberta Funeral Service Association

Allan Hunsperger's book gives excellent insight into what the Bible says about honoring our dead. He has collected and compiled his analysis of the scriptures in a sensitive and sensible method that helps the reader to understand how Christian traditions have influenced our western practices of honoring our dead.

Tyler Weber
President
Alberta Funeral Service Association

Preface

In 2005, I became pastor of a church that had started in March 1928. From its beginning, the church had had a cemetery. It was the first church I had ever been involved with that had a cemetery.

The interesting thing is that, even though it's not the practice of today, we don't ask why it was the practice of churches one hundred years ago.

I made sure the cemetery was looked at, and we maintained it and administrated when someone who wanted to be buried there passed away.

However, when we changed the name of the church, everything changed. Changing the name of the church required changing the name of the cemetery as well.

This change of name was a concern to some the older people of the community who no longer attended the church but had loved ones buried in the cemetery and were planning to be buried there as well.

I am very grateful for these people who challenged me to look into it further to make sure we were doing the right thing.

That was when I began to start to ask myself some questions.

Why would a church have a cemetery? Who should be buried in the cemetery? How do the members of my church feel about the cemetery? What will the future of the cemetery be? What will the new name be?

We began to have designated days in the summer to all meet at the cemetery so we could help people understand why we bury people in cemeteries, why we put their names on memorial stones, and how our children should feel about all of it.

As I began to study for those gatherings, I was shocked at how much scripture there was in the Bible about burials. I began to see what the Bible said about cremation, and I realized all of us would be making decisions about burials someday, and perhaps a little background would help us in that decision. Thus the book, *Final Act of Honor*!

Introduction

I don't know about you, but I had never studied the subject of burials. I knew that, for the most part, we either buried someone in a casket and then put that into a grave with a memorial stone on the top of it, or we cremated the body and either put the ashes in an urn or scattered the ashes over some memorial place.

We don't always know why we do these things. Sometimes we just do them. Sometimes we do it out of tradition. Sometimes we do it because of religion beliefs. Sometimes we do it because of money concerns.

So now you find yourself, maybe for the first time in your life, having to make the decision about what you are going to do with the remains of your loved one.

Even though I had been in the ministry for more than fifty years and had officiated at many funerals, I had never done any kind of research to understand why people make the burial decisions they do and whether or not there is a right way and a wrong way to do it. I was also on a board of directors of a funeral home and found that even those in the business didn't understand the answers to those questions.

Usually, people are thrown into the situation where they have to make a decision about the remains of a loved one, and it is time sensitive, so they don't have time to research what they are about to decide.

This short book will help you with that decision. I purposely designed this to be short because of your time frame to make a decision. It is written to inform and enlighten you as a guide, not to judge or commend you in whatever decision you make.

Hopefully it will help.

Important
Questions to Ask

I don't know if you remember or ever saw the movie *The End of Rocky Balboa*, but at the end of the movie, Rocky is visiting the grave of his beloved wife, Adrian. He puts a dozen roses on the top of the memorial stone, kneels down, and says, "You know I couldn't have done anything without you." He pauses and then says the famous line, "Yo, Adrian, we did it." Rocky then leans forward, kisses the roses, stands up, and begins to leave his very important visit to the love of his life.

The movie ends there, but you get the idea that he's done this before, and it won't be the last time he visits the grave of his wife—a tradition that is being lost in today's culture. Many of us were never taught the importance of burials and the burial place. Nor were we taught the importance of memorial stones and the location of the burial. They can seem like added costs that are unnecessary. After all, no one ever sees the remains again. And maybe no one cares.

Unless, like Rocky, the love of your life has passed away and you can never forget the memories—nor should you. Those memories are a part of you and always will be, good or bad. We learn from both.

Why, then, do we have cemeteries? Why do we bury the remains of our loved ones in a casket and place them in a plot of land? In addition, why do we purchase a memorial stone to be placed at the grave site, with information about the deceased engraved on it?

Why not cremate the body and disperse the ashes to wherever we wish instead of purchasing a plot of land, a casket, and a memorial stone?

Cremation is happening more and more, sometimes without even having a service in honor of the one who has passed. However, we need some background before we make this very important decision. I am sure you will agree with me after you have read this book.

First let's consider a couple of things.

In making our decision, does it just come down to the question of cost? Is disposing of the body an act of convenience and cost, or should it be a matter of honor and lasting remembrance?

Has anyone ever researched the pros and cons of how we are to handle the remains of our loved ones? Should we? Is it important?

Well, we are talking about something that has been done for centuries. Just go for a drive in your city or through the countryside and see if you pass by a cemetery or two—or maybe more.

You will likely pass by more than one cemetery, perhaps including ones you never noticed before when driving. In fact, now when I drive, whether in the city or in the country, I notice them all the time, and I'm surprised by how many there actually are.

So, here again, I ask the question, why? Why, over the centuries, have we developed cemeteries, even in areas of expensive real estate, to bury our dead?

Why do we have national holidays to remember the dead? Remembrance Day, Memorial Day, Good Friday, and D-Day are just a few. Other cultures and religions have their days as well.

I didn't know the answers to these questions because no one ever taught the subject to me, and I'm not sure I really cared or wanted to know.

This is kind of a morbid subject. But should it be?

Was it morbid to me because of my ignorance? My lack of understanding was never a concern because ignorance blinds you from reality and the truth.

As far as I knew, it was tradition. It was what we did when someone passed. I didn't ask why.

Now, when a loved one passes, I have the responsibility of organizing the burial. Should I be ignorant on the subject? What if I don't understand the costs of a funeral and why I should be spending so much money on something I know nothing about?

Is it about finding the most inexpensive way of handling the situation?

Is that how we look at the expense of purchasing a house, or a car, or a vacation, or our education, or the clothes we wear? Do we ask, "What's the most inexpensive house to buy? And the cheapest car to buy? And the most inexpensive clothes?"

Of course not! So why is a burial different? Because we don't know the importance of and reasons for the costs and arrangements for someone who has passed away.

Burials are usually not part of our planning for the future. We know they will happen, but we ignore any planning because it doesn't seem all that important.

Who cares what happens to my body after I'm dead? It just disintegrates. So why spend a lot of money on something that disintegrates over time anyway?

Our Church Has a Cemetery

Even after I first noticed that our church had a cemetery, I still didn't give it much thought. As far as I was concerned, it was more about the responsibility of maintaining it and keeping it organized than anything else. The question of why a church would have a cemetery never entered my mind until the day came when we needed to change the name of the cemetery.

Some of the older people in the community who no longer attended our church but had loved ones buried in the church cemetery were concerned. In my ignorance, I didn't understand why they were concerned. I only knew that they were going to cause trouble if I didn't carefully think through the process of the name change. Today, I am grateful for those people who forced me to look into the importance of burials, burial sites, and cemeteries.

So I needed answers, and I needed them right away!

I went to the scriptures to find the answers to these questions: What does the Bible say about burial and cremation? Does the way I choose to handle my remains matter? Is what the deceased chose important?

Now, I know that some of you reading this book may not believe the Bible, but let me encourage you to continue reading. Remember that the Bible is one of the oldest pieces of literature, and it is still the best-selling book in the world.

After studying the scriptures, as a Christian, I found that there is great importance to what happens with our remains after we pass. In fact, I couldn't believe that, in the Bible, whole chapters are given to the subject of burials. For example, Genesis 23 is about Abraham buying some land so he can bury his wife, Sarah.

I began to wonder, *Why does the Bible give so much attention to burials?*

In my studies, I also found a passage of scripture where some men buried a young man by throwing him on the bones of Elisha the prophet, and the man came back to life. I began to wonder, *What is God trying to tell us about the remains of someone who passes?*

When Jacob was ready to die, he lived in Egypt, and he made he son Joseph swear that his bones would be buried in the burial place of his fathers.

I found it interesting that we have been given details in the Bible about people's private matters, including where to bury their remains.

So the following is for your consideration. There's a lot riding on funeral decisions, and it's not just about finances or convenience or simplicity. It's a decision about honor.

A Decision about Honor

Honor. The original language the Bible was written in was Greek, and the Greek word for honor is *time* (tee-may´): "a value, i.e. money paid, or (concretely and collectively) valuables; by analogy, esteem (especially of the highest degree), or the dignity itself—honour, precious, price, some" (*Greek Strong's Dictionary*).

The first commandment in the Ten Commandments that deals with relationships starts with our relationship with our father and mother. It's the fifth commandment, and it commands us to honor our parents.

> Honour your father and your mother so that you may have a long life in the land that the Lord your God is giving you. (Exodus 20:12)

Notice that it doesn't say, "If your father and mother are honorable, then honor them." It says, "Honor your father and mother," which means honor has to do with *you*, not them. It's not about whether or not they are honorable. It's a question of whether or not you are a person who honors your parents. So honor comes from you.

Similarly, we are encouraged to honor the king. Honor comes from *me*. I give the king honor—whether he is honorable or not.

The opposite of honor is dishonor.

Burying someone without the knowledge of where they are buried and who they are is an act of dishonor. In the Gospel of Luke, Jesus tells the Pharisees that they are like men who have been buried, but because there is no marker to let people know the place where they have been buried, people walk on top of it, which is an act of dishonor.

> Woe to you! *You are like unmarked graves*; the
> people who walk over them don't know it. (Luke
> 11:44; italics added)

This is definitely a figure of speech that Jesus uses to let the scribes and Pharisees know that they are not honored, just like unmarked graves. In fact, they are dead, with no honor given to them by others. These are men who were looking for honor, and no one was giving them the honor they wanted because their graves were unmarked, so people were walking over their graves and not aware of it.

Honor is something we have little understanding about in today's world. We don't often focus on the fact that what we do with the remains of a loved one is an act of honor. However, the more we think about it, the more we can see how it is an act of honor.

I'll never forgot one of my last visits to my mother before she passed away. It was when she knew it wouldn't be long before she left this earth. She started to share with me her wishes in regard to her funeral.

The first thing she said was that she wanted to be cremated. She wanted to know, what did I think?

It just so happened to be a time in my life where I had just studied from the scriptures what the Bible says about burial versus cremation. I was able to show my mother scriptures about the importance of burials and what the scriptures said about cremation.

After I was done sharing with her, her comment to me was, "Well, in light of that, maybe I shouldn't be cremated and should be buried instead." I'm thankful she changed her mind, but I wonder how many people have made a decision about a burial without knowing what the Word of God says about it. And if they did know, would that have changed their decision?

Why Do We Bury a Loved One?

When it comes to burials, your first consideration is *where*. Why would *where* be the first consideration in a burial?

Let's look at the Bible for some answers.

> Now Sarah lived 127 years; these were all the years of her life. Sarah died in Kiriath-arba (that is, Hebron) in the land of Canaan, and Abraham went to mourn for Sarah and to weep for her.
>
> Then Abraham got up from beside his dead wife and spoke to the Hittites: "I am a foreign resident among you. Give me a burial site among you so that I can bury my dead."
>
> The Hittites replied to Abraham, "Listen to us, lord. You are God's chosen one among us. Bury your dead in our finest burial place. None

of us will withhold from you his burial place for burying your dead."

Then Abraham rose and bowed down to the Hittites, the people of the land. He said to them, "If you are willing for me to bury my dead, listen to me and ask Ephron son of Zohar on my behalf to give me the cave of Machpelah that belongs to him; it is at the end of his field. Let him give it to me in your presence, for the full price, as a burial place."

Ephron was sitting among the Hittites. So in the presence of all the Hittites who came to the gate of his city, Ephron the Hittite answered Abraham: "No, my lord. Listen to me. I give you the field, and I give you the cave that is in it. I give it to you in the presence of my people. Bury your dead."

Abraham bowed down to the people of the land and said to Ephron in the presence of the people of the land, "Please listen to me. Let me pay the price of the field. Accept it from me, and let me bury my dead there."

Ephron answered Abraham and said to him, "My lord, listen to me. Land worth 400 shekels of silver—what is that between you and me? Bury your dead." Abraham agreed with Ephron, and Abraham weighed out to Ephron the silver that he had agreed to in the presence of the Hittites: 400 shekels of silver at the current commercial rate. So Ephron's field at Machpelah near Mamre—the field with its cave and all the trees anywhere within the boundaries of the field—became Abraham's possession in the presence of all the Hittites who came to the gate of his city. After this, Abraham buried his wife Sarah in the cave of the field at Machpelah near Mamre (that is, Hebron) in the land of Canaan. The field with its cave passed from the Hittites to Abraham as a burial place. (Genesis 23:1–20)

Why do you think a whole chapter of Genesis is given to informing us what Abraham did after his wife passed away? Could it be God is sharing with us the importance of burials and of the place where we bury our loved ones?

Notice a couple of truths that really stick out when reading this passage of scripture.

Abraham spent some time looking for a good piece of land to purchase, where he would bury his wife. When he found it, he wanted to know the price. He was given an offer that most of us would have accepted, but Abraham turned it down.

The offer—*pick wherever you want and help yourself.* No cost!

The offer was to pick a spot, and it would be his to bury his wife, and the cost would have been nothing.

But notice that Abraham wasn't going to accept the piece of land for nothing. Why not? Why wouldn't Abraham accept the offer and bury his wife in a plot of land that cost him nothing?

Because, to Abraham, the burial of his wife was about more than getting it for free. Burying his wife was an act of honor, and honor has to cost us something in order for it to be worth anything.

He also knew that the burial location was important and that it was an act of honor. So burying her in a foreign land owned by foreigners was not appropriate, unless Abraham purchased the property for the going rate. He, not foreigners, then owned the land where his wife was buried, and he had control of the land where she was buried and where he would later be buried as well.

Notice he bought the land for the current commercial rate. He didn't ask for a reduced rate, even knowing that the owners wanted to give it to him for free.

Genesis 23 is not the only place in scripture where the field that Abraham purchased for his wife is mentioned.

> His sons Isaac and Ishmael buried him in the cave of Machpelah near Mamre, in the field of Ephron son of Zohar the Hittite. This was the field that Abraham bought from the Hittites. Abraham was buried there with his wife Sarah. After Abraham's death, God blessed his son Isaac, who lived near Beer. (Genesis 25:9–10)
>
> Then he commanded them: " I am about to be gathered to my people. Bury me with my fathers in the cave in the field of Ephron the Hittite. The

cave is in the field of Machpelah near Mamre, in the land of Canaan. This is the field Abraham purchased from Ephron the Hittite as a burial site. Abraham and his wife Sarah are buried there, Isaac and his wife Rebekah are buried there, and I buried Leah there. The field and the cave in it were purchased from the Hittites." (Genesis 49:29–32)

Israel settled in the land of Egypt, in the region of Goshen. They acquired property in it and became fruitful and very numerous. Now Jacob lived in the land of Egypt 17 years, and his life span was 147 years. When the time drew near for him to die, he called his son Joseph and said to him, "If I have found favour in your eyes, put your hand under my thigh and promise me that you will deal with me in kindness and faithfulness. Do not bury me in Egypt. When I rest with my fathers, carry me away from Egypt and bury me in their burial place." Joseph answered, "I will do what you have asked." And Jacob said, "Swear to me." So Joseph swore to him. Then Israel bowed in thanks at the head of his bed. (Genesis 47:27–31)

> My father made me take an oath, saying, "I am about to die. You must bury me there in the tomb that I made for myself in the land of Canaan. Now let me go and bury my father. Then I will return." (Genesis 50:5, 13)

> And Jacob went down to Egypt. He and our ancestors died there, were carried back to Shechem, and were placed in the tomb that Abraham had bought for a sum of silver from the sons of Hamor in Shechem. (Acts 7:15–16)

The following are additional scriptures that deal with burials and their importance.

> After these things, the LORD'S servant, Joshua son of Nun, died at the age of 110. They buried him in his allotted territory at Timnath-serah, in the hill country of Ephraim north of Mount Gaash. Israel worshiped Yahweh throughout Joshua's lifetime and during the lifetimes of the elders who outlived Joshua and who had experienced all the works Yahweh had done for Israel.
>
> Joseph's bones, which the Israelites had brought up from Egypt, were buried at Shechem in the parcel of land Jacob had purchased from the sons of Hamor, Shechem's father, for 100 qesitahs. It was an inheritance for Joseph's descendants.
>
> And Eleazar son of Aaron died, and they buried him at Gibeah, which had been given to his son Phinehas in the hill country of Ephraim. (Joshua 24:29–33)

God gives a man riches, wealth, and honor
so that he lacks nothing of all he desires for
himself, but God does not allow him to enjoy
them. Instead, a stranger will enjoy them. This
is futile and a sickening tragedy. A man may
father a hundred children and live many years.
No matter how long he lives, if he is not satisfied
by good things and does not even have a proper
burial, I say that a stillborn child is better off
than he. (Ecclesiastes 6:2–3)

All the kings of the nations lie in splendor,
each in his own tomb. But you are thrown
out without a grave, like a worthless branch,
covered by those slain with the sword and
dumped into a rocky pit like a trampled corpse.
You will not join them in burial, because you
destroyed your land and slaughtered your own
people. The offspring of evildoers will never be
remembered. (Isaiah 14:18–20)

The burial and the location of that burial was important.

Most of the burial sites are places where generations have
been buried. These become historical sites that you can take
your family to. You can show them your family background,
and the memorial stones end up telling the story of your family.

Many today are interested in the DNA of their families and
backgrounds. Burial grounds of generations help tell that story.

So when you're planning a burial site, don't just think about today. Think of generations to come and what they will be able to learn about their family by your burial site.

Some of us have never considered what happens to the remains of our loved ones, and we may end up making decisions for them. We may find ourselves in a situation where we have to make a decision with no finances available. We may have no choice but to do it the least expensive way possible. I think everyone understands that. Sometimes, decisions we don't want to make have to be made, and maybe there is no other way. It does not mean you don't love your family or that you don't want to honor them.

That is the very reason for this book—to help us understand why we do what we do and what is needed in order to prepare for it.

In some cases, our leadership has failed us in not addressing this subject. As a pastor, I have failed those in the past because of my ignorance. That is why I hope this subject can be taught in our educational institutions for the ministry and for those wanting to go into the field of funeral directing.

Whatever you did with the remains of your loved ones, in no way do I suggest they were dishonorable actions. None of us would ever do that. Sometimes, we just didn't know, and funds were not available to handle it differently.

When I use scripture, we are looking at generations passing on the tradition, from one generation to the next. That was lost over the years, and we are now trying to bring it back.

Today, because of our lack of understanding, we may look at burials as an inconvenience or an unnecessary cost to get rid of the remains of someone who has just passed away. We may look for the easiest and cheapest way to handle something that should be very important to us and to following generations. The problem is we just don't know.

For many people today, there is no burial spot, no memorial stone, and no story to tell to future generations. Let's be the generation that stops telling the story of our family. Let's carry the legacy of our families on to the next generation.

Where there is no planning, no forethought, and no investment, we can end up making costly decisions financially, psychologically, and spiritually.

Here again, the purpose of this book is to change that. Let's learn and get it back to what it should be.

Knowing Why Is Very Important

The funeral directors of our nation are seeing people shortcut the process of burying their dead by not having a grieving process, which is so important to the human psyche. As a Christian, I believe that's one important reason scripture gives so much attention to the burial process.

Today, I can go back to Didsbury, Alberta, and visit the graves of my forefathers who came from the United States back in the late eighteen hundreds. To me, it is not only a place of remembrance but one of honor as I proudly read the tombstones of my roots here in Alberta, Canada.

There are even graves of my relatives who passed away either at childbirth or soon after, living only a very short time. To me, that's important. They are not forgotten. It also tells me of the struggles that my ancestors went through during their lifetime.

We plan our career, we plan our life, we plan our families and our relationships, we plan our home purchases, and we plan our retirement, but we don't plan for our burial. It's time we change that and include our burial location and costs, for the entire process is a very important part of life.

Honor Is Not Cheap But Is Very Important

> Once, as the Israelites were burying a man, suddenly they saw a raiding party, so they threw the man into Elisha's tomb. When he touched Elisha's bones, the man revived and stood up! (2 Kings 13:21)

The man the Israelites were burying came to life when his dead body touched the bones of Elisha. Wow!

Why? What is God trying to tell us in this passage?

Well, I'm sure that with an intense study, you could find lots of explanations. My answer is one that I think would be the most general of answers in this important text.

I'm not going to go into all of the reasons why a dead man came to life by touching another man's bones, but what I am going to ask is, Why is this verse in the scripture? Is it showing that our remains still carry who we are? Elisha, for example, was a great prophet, a part of amazing miracles in his day, and then this is mentioned about his bones.

As a believer in scripture, I would conclude that even if I don't understand it all, this verse gives value to the remains of the deceased. It says to me that a person's remains are something we need to consider carefully, with respect to the person and honoring the person's life.

We Need to Give Thought and Investment to the Burial Process

Most funeral homes will work with you and help you with this process. Some offer financial plans that allow you to make payments on a monthly basis, with or without interest.

There are also insurance plans that pay for your funeral costs, and you pay into the plan for a certain period of time. All of this takes forethought and planning your life.

Underlying the importance of a burial place is what happened to Moses.

Where Was Moses Buried?

After all the things I mentioned about the importance of a burial site and how generations can go and learn about their ancestors, in my studies, I found that God buried Moses—and nobody knows where that burial spot is located.

It's kind of interesting that the Bible says we will not know where the remains are for Moses.

> So Moses the servant of the Lord died there in the land of Moab, as the Lord had said. He buried him in the valley in the land of Moab facing Beth-peor, and no one to this day knows where his grave is. (Deuteronomy 34:5–6)

Moses was 120 years old when he died. We know that. He was buried by God himself. Very interesting! And "no one to this day knows where his grave is."

Why? I am not sure. My guess is that God didn't want his burial site turned into a shrine. I'm basing that partly on the fact that the people who Moses led tended to worship idols, such as the golden calf. If you read about that, you find out that they not only worshipped the golden calf, but they worshipped it as their god.

So what that says to me is that, as important as a burial site is for our loved ones, it should never be worshipped.

The interesting part is that his age, the area where he died, and the lack of information about where the burial site is—it's all in the scripture.

Further, Moses's burial site is also mentioned in the New Testament. It's found in the book of Jude.

Yet Michael the archangel, when he was disputing with the Devil in a debate about Moses' body, did not dare bring an abusive condemnation against him but said, "The Lord rebuke you!" (Jude 1:9)

Now I would love to get into this verse and give you some of the conjectures of what this verse is all about, but one thing for sure is that this burial site is important and that only God knows where it is. Even the devil doesn't know its location. He wanted to know where, but Michael the archangel wasn't giving it to him. Or maybe Michael the archangel doesn't even know. Some think that Michael the archangel was the one who buried Moses. For now, we will stick to what the verse in Deuteronomy says, which is He (God) buried Moses.

To me, that is the most interesting part of this scripture. God buried Moses.

Because this burial is mentioned in the scripture, and God did the burial, a burial must be very important to God. And if that is true, which I believe it is, then the burials of our loved ones *must* be important to us.

Now there's so much more to learn, but what I have given you is the most important basics about burials and some very important reasons why you need to understand this process. We should not be looking for the easiest way or the cheapest way but for the proper way, the biblical way, the way that God intended for us—the honorable way!

Memorial Stones

How many times have you heard someone say, "Well, you can't take it with you," referring to the things that we acquire while living on this planet?

I'm going to ask you, What can we leave behind that will be lasting over the generations?

Memorial stones are very important in that they tell a brief story of the person who is buried. We must remember that this memorial stone is something for future generations. Much thought needs to be put into a memorial stone.

There are so many creative ways of telling your story, so you need to get with someone who can guide you through this process. But first, let's look at the scripture and see the use of memorial stones.

> After the entire nation had finished crossing the Jordan, the Lord spoke to Joshua: "Choose 12 men from the people, one man for each tribe,

and command them: Take 12 stones from this place in the middle of the Jordan where the priests are standing, carry them with you, and set them down at the place where you spend the night."

So Joshua summoned the 12 men he had selected from the Israelites, one man for each tribe, and said to them, "Go across to the ark of the Lord your God in the middle of the Jordan. Each of you lift a stone onto his shoulder, one for each of the Israelite tribes, so that this will be a sign among you. In the future, when your children ask you, 'What do these stones mean to you?' you should tell them, 'The waters of the Jordan were cut off in front of the ark of the Lord's covenant. When it crossed the Jordan, the Jordan's waters were cut off. Therefore these stones will always be a memorial for the Israelites.'"

The Israelites did just as Joshua had commanded them. The 12 men took stones from the middle of the Jordan, one for each of the Israelite tribes, just as the Lord had told Joshua. They carried them to the camp and set them down there. Joshua also set up 12 stones in the middle of the Jordan where the priests who carried the ark of the covenant were standing. The stones are there to this day. (Joshua 4:1–9)

To me, the most striking part of this is when the Israelites were given the reason for building a pile of twelve stones in the middle of the Jordan.

Here's the quote: "In the future, when your children ask you, 'What do these stones mean to you?' you should tell them ..."

Wow! I love this. *When your children ask you.* That's the reason God gave to them, the answer to the why.

What happens in the now can help future generations. The problem is that when we are buying a loved one, we might only think of our grief and not about future generations that will be interested in knowing about past generations.

We might even think that we are not important and that future generations wouldn't care or won't want to know about us. But this passage is saying the opposite. Future generations will ask questions about their ancestors—which you and I become in the future.

Cemeteries and memorial stones carry importance far beyond our immediate generation. Who would have thought that giving a sample of our DNA and seeing where our ancestry came from was going to be a fad? Billions of dollars have been spent on this because people are hungry to know their roots and who is in those roots. It helps them know who they are. Your memorial stone plays a part in this. That is why it is so important.

Generations that will follow you will want to know who you are, when and where you were born, when and where you died, if you got married, and if so, to whom. These are the basics, and you can be as creative as you want to be with your memorial stone, adding to your story.

Each of us should be making our own memorial stone long before we pass away and not leaving it to our loved ones to do. Rarely does this happen, but maybe your reading this book will begin to change that.

Look at Deuteronomy 27:1–8:

> Moses and the elders of Israel commanded the people, "Keep every command I am giving you today. At the time you cross the Jordan into the land the Lord your God is giving you, you must set up large stones and cover them with plaster. Write all the words of this law on the stones after you cross to enter the land the Lord your God is giving you, a land flowing with milk and honey, as Yahweh, the God of your fathers, has promised you. When you have crossed the Jordan, you are to set up these stones on Mount Ebal, as I am commanding you today, and you are to cover them with plaster. Build an altar of stones there to the Lord your God—you must not use any iron tool on them. Use uncut stones to build the altar of the Lord your God and offer burnt offerings to the Lord your God on it. There you are to sacrifice fellowship offerings, eat, and rejoice in the presence of the Lord your God. Write clearly all the words of this law on the plastered stones."

Here in Deuteronomy 27, God is giving clear instructions for building a memorial, including how to prepare it and what to write on it.

Here again, passing on the law to future generations is the reason for the stones covered with plaster.

And finally on this subject, Cornelius, a roman soldier, was very generous, and his acts of charity became a memorial offering before God. In other words, God remembered his acts of charity because they became a memorial on his behalf.

> Looking intently at him, he became afraid and said, "What is it, lord?" The angel told him, "Your prayers and your acts of charity have come up as a memorial offering before God. (Acts 10:4)

> Cornelius replied, "Four days ago at this hour, at three in the afternoon, I was praying in my house. Just then a man in a dazzling robe stood before me and said, 'Cornelius, your prayer has been heard, and your acts of charity have been remembered in God's sight.'" (Acts 10:31–32)

So now that you know all this, what's your plan?

Some may say it is not fair to those who don't have extra money or enough money, that this act of honor costs money, so it's only for the rich. I believe that is not true.

Life is a choice about priorities! If you need or want

something, you can get it. I may be asking you to stretch your thinking, and please don't say you can't, because I believe you can, and you will—if this is important to you.

Where there is a will, there is a way! I believe that! I'm asking you to believe that as well. It can be hard to believe in something that you think is impossible, but nothing is impossible.

If you begin to work on your burial site and your memorial stone and start saving funds when you begin your life in the work force—a little bit at a time, toward the cost of all this— you will be honored for generations to come, and it will not be a burden to the loved ones you leave behind.

Maybe your loved one has just passed away, and you're left with a decision. You need to make plans for a burial within a very short period of time, and you have no extra funds to do anything but the least expensive plan for burial.

Acts of honor cost us; there's no way of getting around that! Everything I have ever read, heard, and watched suggests that honor costs something. It can even cost your life, depending on the situation—on the battlefield, for example.

And let me add here that every funeral home wants to help you, and many have plans that you can apply to your situation. Just ask.

Now, whether or not you do this or you leave it to your loved ones, a burial site needs to be chosen with some thought for future generations. Plus, your memorial stone needs to be done as well.

I personally never thought about all of this until my wife of fifty years passed away, and then I had to answer the questions that I'm asking you today.

I had done no planning, as it wasn't even in my thoughts. I wish it had been, but that's history. I needed to bury my wife in a proper burial site and place on her site a proper memorial stone.

Yes, the costs were there, but the money wasn't. With all the other expenses that I had and my responsibly to honor my most loved wife, whom I miss to this day, I had to fulfil my duty. There were no other options—unless I don't care about honor. And if I don't care about honor, that means I'm not a person of honor. Do I want to leave that to my future generations? No, I don't. So God would help me fulfill my duty to my lovely wife, Lucinda Sue, and then prepare for my own passing so that my passing doesn't become a burden on my loved ones.

And perhaps that's the number one reason I'm writing this book—to help you and your family be prepared so that your legacy will carry on from generation to generation.

Memorial stones establish generational honor that can affect future generations.

Cremation

Now, the following is not intended to make those of you who have chosen to cremate your loved ones feel guilty in any way. What you did for your loved one(s) was honorable, and I know it came from a heart of love.

I am only showing you what it says in the Bible, but you have to make your own choices in life. God gave that to humans from the very beginning. I would never judge you or condemn what you did or plan to do. I love you, and I feel sorrow with you for your loss. Having lost the love of my life, I understand grief and grieving. I have experienced both. My wife passed away on October 10, 2019, and there are times when I still find tears filling my eyes and running down my cheeks. There are times when I feel lonely and wish things could have been different. But life is what it is, and I need to move forward with a life that brings honor to her memory.

So I am bringing to your attention these scriptures in the Bible about the burning of a body only for your information and nothing else. My prayer is not to hide anything but to give us all credit that we can work through our own thoughts and make plans from there.

Nowhere in scripture does it say not to use cremation as a way of handling the remains of your loved ones. If fact, that's how some cultures do all of their burials. And usually, great honor is given in these rituals of different cultures. I'm just showing you what the Bible says.

It's a temptation for me not to write this part of the book because I don't want anyone to feel guilty about what has happened in the past.

God loves you, and I love you, and you acted or are acting out of love, based on what you were told or encouraged to do by others.

I remember hearing a message on the radio by a very popular radio pastor who said the Bible does not say, "Thou shalt not cremate." I have never forgotten that.

However, in my study on this subject, I was forced to look into what the Bible does say about cremation, if anything. What I found was the following material, and you can draw your own conclusions.

So let's move to what seems to be the most popular practice of our day—cremation.

Cremation is not really an option in the scriptures. It's true that scripture does not say, "Thou shalt not cremate"; however, there is the burning of the remains of the dead in scripture.

Before we go any further, I want to give you some truth about the burning of bodies as a pagan practice in scripture, worshiping other gods.

Molech was a Canaanite god associated with death and the underworld. The worshipping ritual of passing someone through fire was connected with him. This ritual could have been either fire walking or child sacrifice (Thayer), but it entailed a form of worship to this Canaanite god, mostly with children.

> You are not to make any of your children pass through the fire to Molech. Do not profane the name of your God; I am Yahweh. (Leviticus 18:21)

> Say to the Israelites: Any Israelite or foreigner living in Israel who gives any of his children to Molech must be put to death; the people of the country are to stone him. (Leviticus 20:2)

> They have built the high places of Baal in the Valley of Hinnom to make their sons and daughters pass through the fire to Molech— something I had not commanded them. I had never entertained the thought that they do this detestable act causing Judah to sin! (Jeremiah 32:35)

My point is burning a body was a form of worship to the pagan god Molech. That alone should at least cause us to pause and ask, Why do we think burning the remains of a loved one is proper? Where did it come from?

Well, I can tell you it didn't come from God, who created us. He gave us scripture that shares what is to be done with the remains of a loved one.

Has the worship of a pagan god crept into our society through our ignorance in the practice of cremation? I'm not making that conclusion as a definite statement, but I am sharing this for us to do some thinking on the matter.

There is an interesting story in Genesis 38 about Judah and Tamar, and in verse 24, it says the following:

> About three months later Judah was told, "Your daughter-in-law, Tamar, has been acting like a prostitute, and now she is pregnant."
>
> "Bring her out!" Judah said. "Let her be burned to death!"

Now Tamar never was burned to death, because the one who got her pregnant was Judah, and Tamar could prove it.

My point is Judah's response to finding out that his daughter-in-law was acting like a prostitute and was pregnant. His judgment on her was one of dishonor, even though he, too, was a man of dishonor. It was a death sentence of burning versus handling the remains, but you see the point of the thought of burning.

Generally speaking, cremation is a trend in today's culture. Those who help and counsel those grieving are concerned about how today's society is not dealing with grief.

Many church groups have a program called Grief Share, where those who have lost a loved one meet with others who have also lost a loved one for about a year, which is helping many.

There's very little thought today about the grieving process. There's no thought about remembering our dead from one generation to the next—no thought of honor or dishonor.

You and I both know that this subject of what to do when someone passes on is usually something we do not really think about much—until we are forced to make these decisions for either ourselves or others.

So scripture shows that burning the bones was a way to dispose of the remains, but there is no—or at least very little—honor there. It was usually in disgrace, punishment, and/or judgment of someone evil. Even when scriptures mention someone who was burned to death because of their evil acts, their bones were still taken and buried with a marker of remembrance.

This is not something we like to talk about, but it's something we need to talk about, think about, and plan for.

Burying is not only an act of honor but also leaves a memorial to be viewed by future generations. Therefore, memorial stones are a very important part of burial.

A memorial stone is not only a marker stating a location; it's also a reminder of generations past for family members, friends, and the world to see.

Every human has given something positive to this world.

Every human is important to Father God and should also be important to family and friends for years to come.

Maybe we didn't find a cure for a terrible disease or built a historical structure, but we did play a role in a life or lives that benefits future generations. It may be small or large, but it really doesn't matter. Future generations are here today because of the generations in our past.

All of us can learn from one another, and that learning doesn't stop upon our death. It carries on to future generations.

My Thoughts for You Experiencing the Loss of a Loved One

You will miss your loved one who has just passed for the rest of your life. Right now, your grief is at its highest level, and it will change over time, but you memory of your loved one will never be lost.

I have lost my parents, my older sister and younger brother, and now my wife of fifty years. I'm the only family member left, so I understand loss.

Some struggle more than others in the grieving process, and as I mentioned, there are grief share groups available to help you. However, it's never easy. Don't hold back your tears. Don't feel ashamed by your grief.

Share your memories about your loved one any time with anyone. It helps every time you share those memories.

If you have a favorite song that you and your loved one enjoyed together, play it.

Guard yourself against self-pity by finding a close friend that you can call at any time to share what's happening with you. It may be a family member, a friend, your pastor/priest, or whoever you feel comfortable sharing your sorrow with.

It doesn't matter who comes into your life from this point on. Your loved one will always be with you.

Printed in the United States
by Baker & Taylor Publisher Services